Doll
Hair

FOR GIRLS WHO LOVE TO
STYLE THEIR DOLLS' HAIR!

by Emily Osborn

★ American Girl®

Published by American Girl Publishing

No part of this book may be reproduced in any manner
whatsoever without written permission except in the case of
brief quotations embodied in critical articles and reviews.

19 20 21 22 23 24 QP 10 9 8 7 6 5 4 3 2 1

Editorial Development: Emily Osborn
Art Direction and Design: Gretchen Becker
Production: Jeannette Bailey, Kristi Lively, Cynthia Stiles
Photography: Joe Hinrichs, Derek Brabender, Chris Kessler
Set Styling: Kim Sphar
Doll Styling: Kelly Erickson, Tanya McCoy
Illustrations: Monika Roe

Even though instructions have been tested and results
from testing have been incorporated into this book, all
recommendations and suggestions are made without any
guarantees on the part of American Girl. Because of differing
tools, materials, ingredients, conditions, and individual skills, the
publisher disclaims liability for any injuries, losses, or damages
that may result from using the information in this book. Not all
craft materials are tested to the same standards as toy products.

Do you love to play with your doll's hair, creating fun styles to fit the occasion? Now you can treat your doll to a salon style without leaving your room! You can practice the basics—ponytails, braids, and buns—until they're a snap. You can use the kit's comb to keep your doll's hair in shape. Use the styles in this book for any event. Try the high ponytail at a barbecue or the double bun at a bowling party. Watch the how-to hairstyle videos at americangirl. com/play ▶. Practice your skills, and create fun 'dos of your own design!

Have fun stylin'!

YOUR FRIENDS AT AMERICAN GIRL

Hairstyle Helpers ▶

- Keep your doll still. Sit her between your legs, or ask someone to hold her.

- Always use a wire doll hairbrush for styling. If your doll has curly hair, use a hair pick. Plastic bristles snag and frizz doll hair.

- For best styling results, lightly mist your doll's hair with water. Then take a short section at the tip and work your way toward the scalp.

- Never get your doll wet. Protect her face and body from water. Cover her with a plastic cape or a towel, and hold your hand over her eyes when misting.

- Don't pull your doll's hair too hard when brushing, or her neck could come loose. If you can, hold her neck as you work.

- Never use a blow-dryer, hot rollers, curling iron, or straightening iron on your doll's hair. A doll's hair is made of a special acrylic, and any heat source will frizz or melt it.

Emergency Wash ▶

Washing your doll's hair too often can frizz and weaken it. So save the washes for accidents with dripping ice cream or mud splatters. Instead, gently run a wet washcloth down the length of the soiled hair. If you must wash, follow these steps:

1. Cover your doll's eyes with a towel. Tip her head back under the faucet, and wet her hair with cool water. Make sure she's faceup so that the water flows away from her eyes.

2. Gently lather her hair with a mild shampoo, and then rinse until the water runs clear.

3. Lay the doll down with her head on a dry towel. Wrap the towel around her head, squeezing out excess water. Do not twist or rub!

4. Remove tangles from the ends to the roots so that you don't pull out hair. Let dry overnight, or for quicker drying, place your doll in front of a cool fan—but never use a hair dryer.

Basic Ponytails

1. Plain Ponytail

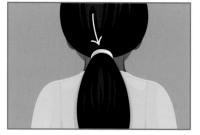

1. Pull your doll's hair to the back of her head. Smooth out loose strands with a brush while holding the hair in your other hand.

2. Wrap on an elastic, twisting the elastic for a second or third wrap. Make the ponytail as high on your doll's head as you like.

3. High Ponytail
Try a high ponytail by pulling all the hair to the crown and wrapping with an elastic.

2. Ponytail Wrap

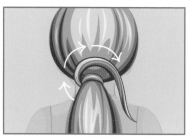

1. Make a low ponytail, leaving a small strand of hair underneath the tail out of the elastic.

2. Wrap the loose strand around the elastic one or two times, depending on your doll's hair length.

3. Tip the doll upside down, tuck the rest of the loose strand into the elastic under the ponytail, and pull through.

2.

1.

3.

Intermediate Ponytails

1. **Half Side Ponytail** ▶

If your doll doesn't already have a side part, use the **kit's comb** to create one. Then gather a small section of hair in front on the side opposite the part, and tie off with an elastic.

2. **Side Ponytail**

Gather your doll's hair on one side and tie it off with an elastic.

3. **Game-Time Ponytail**

Make a half ponytail and tie off with an elastic. About halfway down the half ponytail, add another elastic. Gather the half ponytail with the rest of your doll's hair to create one big ponytail. Tie off with an elastic.

ADVANCED PONYTAILS

1. Ponytail Flip ▶

Gather your doll's hair into a low ponytail, and tie off with an elastic. Reach underneath the ponytail and use your finger and thumb to make a hole in the middle of the hair above the elastic. With your other hand, twist the ponytail, grab it with the fingers that are making the hole, and pull it through.

2. Ponytail Veil ▶

1. Start with three half ponytails, one on each side and one in the middle.

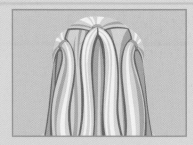

2. Separate the middle ponytail into two sections.

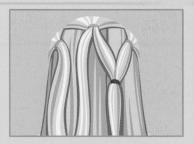

3. Combine the right-hand section with the ponytail on the right, and tie off with an elastic.

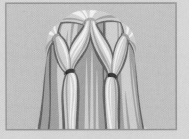

4. Combine the left-hand section with the ponytail on the left, and tie off with an elastic.

5. Bring the two new ponytails to the center and make one big ponytail. Tie off with an elastic.

Basic Braids

1. Single Braid

Gather your doll's hair into a low ponytail. Separate the ponytail into three equal sections. Cross the section on your right over the center section. Cross the section on your left over the center section. Continue crossing over the center section with the right and left sections until the hair is braided. Tie off with an elastic.

2. Half Side Braid

Gather your doll's hair into a half ponytail on the side of her head. Tie off with an elastic, and braid the ponytail. Tie it off with another elastic and add a ribbon if you'd like.

3. Double Braids

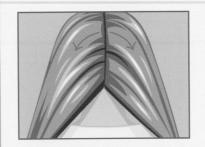

1. Make a part down the back of your doll's head.

2. Tie off one side into a pigtail. Separate the hair on the other side into three equal sections.

3. Cross the section on your right over the center section.

4. Cross the section on your left over the center section.

5. Continue crossing over the center section with right and left sections until hair is braided. Tie off with an elastic. Repeat on the other side.

Tip: Keep a tight hold on sections as you cross them.

Intermediate Braids

1. Two Half Braids

Gather a small section of hair on one side of your doll's head. Braid the section and tie off with an elastic. Repeat on the other side.

2. French Braid

1. Gather hair from the front of your doll's head and separate it into three even sections.

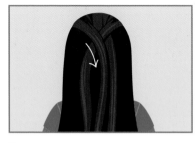

2. Begin by crossing over the right and left sections once, as you would for a regular braid.

3. Grab a few strands of hair to the right of the braid and add them to the right-hand section. Cross the section over the center.

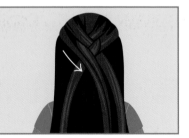

4. Grab a few strands of hair to the left of the braid and add them to the left-hand section. Cross the section over the center.

5. Repeat steps 3 and 4 until all hair has been added; then continue with a regular braid. Tie off with an elastic.

1.

2.

1. Half Ponytail Braid ▶

Gather your doll's hair into a half ponytail in the center of her head, and tie off with an elastic. Braid the ponytail, tie it off with another elastic, and add a ribbon if you'd like.

3. Double Fishtail Braids

Try two fishtail braids. Make a part down the back of your doll's head for pigtails, and follow the fishtail braid instructions for each side.

2. Fishtail Braid

1. Gather your doll's hair into a low ponytail, and tie off with an elastic. Divide the ponytail into two equal parts.

2. Separate a half-inch section of hair from the outside left of the ponytail. Pull this piece across the top of the left ponytail over to the right ponytail.

3. Separate a half-inch section of hair from the outside right of the ponytail. Pull this piece across the top of the right ponytail over to the left ponytail.

4. Repeat steps 2 and 3 until the hair is braided. Tie off with an elastic, and add a ribbon if you'd like.

Basic Buns

1. Classic Bun

1. Gather your doll's hair at the back of her head, and make a high ponytail. Tie off with an elastic.

2. Twist the ponytail tightly, spritzing it with water to keep shorter ends from popping out.

3. Wrap the twisted ponytail around and around the elastic.

4. Tuck the end of the ponytail under the bun, and insert a hairpin or bobby pin to hold it in place.

5. Pin the rest of the bun in place, crisscrossing pins and grabbing hair from the scalp and bun.

2. Low Bun
Try a low bun by making a low ponytail and following the classic bun instructions.

Intermediate Buns

1. **Low Side Bun**

Gather your doll's hair into a low side pony-tail. Tie off with an elastic. Tie the ponytail into a big knot around the elastic.

2. **Messy Bun**

Gather your doll's hair into a high ponytail. Tie off with an elastic. Very loosely pin the ends of the ponytail around the elastic.

Advanced Buns

1. Double Bun

Gather your doll's hair into two high pigtails, and tie them off with elastics. Starting on one side, twist a pigtail until it coils up, and tuck the end underneath the coil. Insert hairpins into the coil, crisscrossing them. Repeat on the other side.

2. Curly Top Bun

This style works only on dolls with short, curly hair. Gather your doll's hair into a high ponytail. Tie off with an elastic. Spread hair around the elastic.

3. Mouse Ears

1. Gather your doll's hair into two high pigtails, and tie them off with elastics.

2. For one ear, add a second elastic and tuck half the pigtail through to create a loop.

3. Wrap the other end of the pigtail around the back and pull through the loop. Use a hairpin to secure the end into the elastics.

4. Carefully spread the looped hair over the tucked hair to create an ear shape. Secure the ends with hairpins. Repeat on the other side.

Basic Pigtails

1. Plain Pigtails

If your doll doesn't already have a center part, make one with the **kit's comb.** The part should extend all the way down the back of her head. Gather the hair on one side, and tie off with an elastic. Repeat on the other side.

2. Half Pigtails

If your doll doesn't already have a center part, make one with the **kit's comb.** Gather a small section of hair on one side of the part, and tie off with an elastic. Repeat on the other side.

3. High Pigtails

Follow the instructions for plain pigtails, gathering the hair high on your doll's head.

1.

2.

Advanced Pigtails

1. Bun Puffs

This style works only on dolls with shorter, curly hair. Gather your doll's hair into two high pigtails, and tie them off with elastics. Spread your doll's hair around the elastics.

2. Star Pigtails

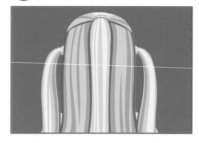

1. Make three small half pony-tails, one on either side of your doll's head and one on top.

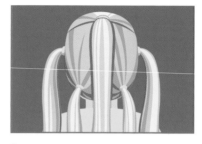

2. Make two low pigtails with the remaining hair.

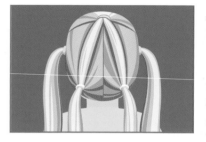

3. Separate the top ponytail in half. Use two new elastics to attach each half to the low pigtails.

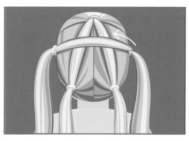

4. Cross half of the right pony-tail to the left, and use an elastic to attach it to the left ponytail.

5. Cross the remainder of the right ponytail down to the left pigtail and attach it with an elastic.

6. Cross the left ponytail down to the right pigtail and attach it with an elastic. Add hair ribbons if you'd like.

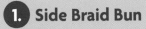

FANCY 'DOS

1. Side Braid Bun

1. Gather your doll's hair into a low side ponytail, leaving a 2-inch section in the front.

2. French-braid the 2-inch section. Tie off with an elastic.

3. Twist the braid until it coils around itself.

4. Tuck the end of the ponytail under the coil, or bun, and insert a hairpin to hold it in place.

2. Headband Tuck

1. Place a hair ribbon elastic around your doll's head.

2. Gently tuck pieces of your doll's hair a little bit at a time into the elastic, starting at the front.

3. Continue around your doll's head until all the hair is tucked into the elastic.

FUN TWISTS

1. **Rope Braid**

Gather your doll's hair into two pigtails, and tie them off with elastics. Separate one pigtail into two equal sections. Tightly cross one section over the other until you reach the end of the pigtail. Tie off with an elastic. Repeat on the other side.

2. **Crown Braid**

Start by making low double braids. Gently pull on the braids to loosen them a bit. Secure each braid on top of your doll's head with hairpins.

Send it in!

What is your doll's favorite hairstyle? To tell us, write to:

Doll Hair **Editor**
American Girl
8400 Fairway Place
Middleton, WI 53562

(Sorry, but photos can't be returned. All comments and suggestions received by American Girl may be used without compensation or acknowledgment.)

Here are some other American Girl®
activity books you might like:

Each sold separately. Find more books online at americangirl.com.

Parents, request a FREE catalogue at **americangirl.com/catalogue**.
Sign up at **americangirl.com/email** to receive the latest news and exclusive offers.

play@
☆American Girl™

Discover online games, quizzes, activities,
and more at **americangirl.com**